N. T. WRIGHT
FOR EVERYONE
BIBLE STUDY GUIDES

EPHESIANS

11 STUDIES FOR INDIVIDUALS AND GROUPS

N. T. WRIGHT

WITH LIN JOHNSON

IVP Connect

An imprint of InterVarsity Press
Downers Grove, Illinois

InterVarsity Press
P.O. Box 1400, Downers Grove, IL 60515-1426
World Wide Web: www.ivpress.com
E-mail: email@ivpress.com

This study guide is based on and includes excerpts adapted from Paul for Everyone: The Prison Letters, ©2002, 2004 Nicholas Thomas Wright. All Scripture quotations, unless otherwise indicated, are taken from the New Testament for Everyone. Copyright ©2001-2008 by Nicholas Thomas Wright. Used by permission of SPCK, London. All rights reserved.

InterVarsity Press® is the book-publishing division of InterVarsity Christian Fellowship/USA®, a movement of students and faculty active on campus at hundreds of universities, colleges and schools of nursing in the United States of America, and a member movement of the International Fellowship of Evangelical Students. For information about local and regional activities, write Public Relations Dept., InterVarsity Christian Fellowship/USA, 6400 Schroeder Rd., P.O. Box 7895, Madison, WI 53707-7895, or visit the IVCF website at <www.intervarsity.org>.

Design: Cindy Kiple
Cover image: Michal Affanasowicz/Trevillion Images
Interior image: Clipart.com

ISBN 978-0-8308-2190-7

Printed in the United States of America ∞

| P | 19 | 18 | 17 | 16 | 15 | 14 | 13 | 12 | 11 | 10 | 9 | 8 | 7 | 6 | 5 | 4 | 3 |
| Y | 25 | 24 | 23 | 22 | 21 | 20 | 19 | 18 | 17 | 16 | 15 | 14 | 13 | 12 | 11 | | |

CONTENTS

GETTING THE MOST
OUT OF EPHESIANS

The most successful tourist attraction to appear in London in recent years is the London Eye. From a distance it looks like a giant Ferris wheel, but this is no fun-fair ride. For a start, it's far, far bigger: it rises to 450 feet above the River Thames. Its thirty-two capsules can each hold twenty people, and it takes them half an hour to rotate the full circle. Plenty of time to have a wonderful view of all central London, with its historic buildings and palaces, its cathedrals and abbeys, its parks and gardens, with Big Ben and the Houses of Parliament in the foreground. The London Eye is, in fact, not only a wonderful sight in itself, visible from many points in the capital. It is the place from which you can get the best possible view of London. To do any better, you'd have to go up in an airplane, and indeed it is operated and run by one of the airline companies.

The letter to the Ephesians stands in relation to the rest of Paul's letters rather like the London Eye does to the rest of the capital. It isn't the longest or fullest of his writing, but it offers a breathtaking view of the entire landscape. From here, as the wheel turns, you get a bird's-eye view of one theme after another within early Christian reflection: God, the world, Jesus, the church, the means of salvation, Christian behavior, marriage and the family, and spiritual warfare. Like someone used to strolling around London and now suddenly able to see familiar places from unfamiliar angles—and to see more easily how they relate to each other within the city as a whole—the reader who comes to Ephesians after reading the rest of Paul will get a new angle on the way in which his thinking holds together.

This letter was originally intended as a circular to various churches in the Ephesus area. It was written around A.D. 60-62 while Paul, the apostle to the Gentiles, was in a Roman prison. (For an account of how Saul of Tarsus became Paul, a believer in Jesus the Messiah, read Acts 9:1-31.) A copy of this letter might well have remained in the possession of the church in Ephesus, and someone later on might have assumed that it was written *to* Ephesus rather than from there.

Since in Colossians—which is very similar to Ephesians in many ways—Paul says that he's sending a letter to Laodicea which will be passed on to them, it's clear he did indeed sometimes write circular letters. The present letter might even be that "letter to Laodicea," though we can't now be sure of that. And at the start of chapter 3 of the present letter, Paul seems to be talking to various people who don't know him and his work firsthand—which would hardly have applied in Ephesus itself, where he spent a long time (Acts 19). If we suppose that he intended the letter to go to several young churches within a hundred miles or so of Ephesus, we shan't go far wrong. (For more on this letter, also see my *Paul for Everyone: The Prison Letters,* on which this guide is based, published by SPCK and Westminster John Knox.)

As we study Ephesians in this guide, prepared with the help of Lin Johnson for which I am grateful, we look to be strengthened and encouraged as Christians for the new tasks that lie ahead. We should also remember that all genuine Christian life and action flows out of worship. True worship of the true God cannot help telling and retelling, with joy and amazement, the story of what this God has done in Jesus the Messiah. Enjoy the view. You won't get a better one.

SUGGESTIONS FOR INDIVIDUAL STUDY

1. As you begin each study, pray that God will speak to you through his Word.

2. Read the introduction to the study and respond to the "Open" question that follows it. This is designed to help you get into the theme of the study.

3. Read and reread the Bible passage to be studied. Each study is designed to help you consider the meaning of the passage in its context. The commentary and questions in this guide are based on my own translation of each passage found in the companion volume to this guide in the For Everyone series on the New Testament (published by SPCK and Westminster John Knox).

4. Write your answers to the questions in the spaces provided or in a personal journal. Each study includes three types of questions: observation questions, which ask about the basic facts in the passage; interpretation questions, which delve into the meaning of the passage; and application questions, which help you discover the implications of the text for growing in Christ. Writing out your responses can bring clarity and deeper understanding of yourself and of God's Word.

5. Each session features selected comments from the For Everyone series. These notes provide further biblical and cultural background and contextual information. They are designed not to answer the questions for you but to help you along as you study the Bible for yourself. For even more reflections on each passage, you may wish to have on hand a copy of the companion volume from the For Everyone series as you work through this study guide.

6. Use the guidelines in the "Pray" section to focus on God, thanking him for what you have learned and praying about the applications that have come to mind.

SUGGESTIONS FOR GROUP MEMBERS

1. Come to the study prepared. Follow the suggestions for individual study mentioned above. You will find that careful preparation will greatly enrich your time spent in group discussion.

2. Be willing to participate in the discussion. The leader of your group

will not be lecturing. Instead, she or he will be asking the questions found in this guide and encouraging the members of the group to discuss what they have learned.

3. Stick to the topic being discussed. These studies focus on a particular passage of Scripture. Only rarely should you refer to other portions of the Bible or outside sources. This allows for everyone to participate on equal ground and for in-depth study.

4. Be sensitive to the other members of the group. Listen attentively when they describe what they have learned. You may be surprised by their insights! Each question assumes a variety of answers. Many questions do not have "right" answers, particularly questions that aim at meaning or application. Instead the questions push us to explore the passage more thoroughly.

   When possible, link what you say to the comments of others. Also, be affirming whenever you can. This will encourage some of the more hesitant members of the group to participate.

5. Be careful not to dominate the discussion. We are sometimes so eager to express our thoughts that we leave too little opportunity for others to respond. By all means participate! But allow others to also.

6. Expect God to teach you through the passage being discussed and through the other members of the group. Pray that you will have an enjoyable and profitable time together, but also that as a result of the study you will find ways that you can take action individually and/or as a group.

7. It will be helpful for groups to follow a few basic guidelines. These guidelines, which you may wish to adapt to your situation, should be read at the beginning of the first session.

   • Anything said in the group is considered confidential and will not be discussed outside the group unless specific permission is given to do so.

   • We will provide time for each person present to talk if he or she feels comfortable doing so.

- We will talk about ourselves and our own situations, avoiding conversation about other people.

- We will listen attentively to each other.

- We will be very cautious about giving advice.

Additional suggestions for the group leader can be found at the back of the guide.

1

BLESSINGS FROM GOD

Ephesians 1:1-14

Have you noticed how sometimes you have a story in the back of your mind which keeps peeping out even when you're talking about something else?

Imagine you've come back from work and the bus has been late again. You stood for half an hour on the station platform getting cold and cross. Then when it arrived it was so full of people you had to stand, uncomfortably, all the way home.

But when you tell your family or friends about the trip you find you're also telling them a larger story. Everybody knows the buses aren't running properly because the present government has allowed the system to get worse and worse. But there's an election coming soon, and then you'll be able to vote out this government and put in another one that might get you decent bus service.

So as you talk about your anger over this evening's ride, you are talking as well about your anger with the present government. And as you talk about how things could be better with the bus you normally catch, you are talking as well about how good things are going to be with the new government. There is a larger framework, a larger story, within which your own smaller stories become more interesting and important.

OPEN

When have you heard of or done something like this—telling someone about an ordinary event and linking it to a larger issue? If not, what might it remind you of in your own life?

STUDY

1. *Read Ephesians 1:1-10.* Paul's great prayer at the opening of this letter is a celebration of the larger story within which every single Christian story—every story of individual conversion, faith, spiritual life, obedience and hope—is set. Only by understanding and celebrating the larger story can we hope to understand everything that's going on in our own smaller stories, and so observe God at work in and through our own lives. Before Paul tells the story, however, he introduces himself.

   Why does Paul start with his credentials (vv. 1-2)?

2. Before Paul will even come to a report of his specific prayers, he establishes what is after all the appropriate context for all Christian prayer, reflection and exhortation: the worship and adoration of the God who has lavished his love upon us. Why is God to be worshiped and adored in this way (vv. 2-3)?

3. What has God done for us in and through Jesus the Messiah?

4. What does it mean to be chosen by grace (vv. 4-6)?

5. We aren't chosen for our own sake, but for the sake of what God wants to accomplish through us. In what ways might God want to bless (or how is he already blessing) others through you or your Christian community?

6. What blessings have we received in Jesus (vv. 7-8)?

7. Paul says God gives us these blessings lavishly. How closely does "lavishly" fit the way you understand or experience God's attitude toward you? Explain.

8. What is God's big plan (vv. 9-10)?

9. How do you see the beginnings of this plan unfolding today?

Paul tells the story of the cross of Jesus in such a way that we can hear, underneath it, the ancient Jewish story of Passover. Passover was the night when the angel of death came through the land of Egypt, and the blood of the lamb sprinkled on the doorposts rescued the Israelites from the judgment that would otherwise have fallen on them. Telling the story like this—the story of Jesus the Messiah, and the meaning of his death, told in such a way as to bring out the fact that it's the fulfillment of the Exodus story—is a classic Jewish way of celebrating the goodness of God. Worship, for Christians, will almost always involve *telling the story* of what God has done in and through Jesus.

10. *Read Ephesians 1:11-14.* What is our promised inheritance (v. 11)?

11. How do we know we will receive this inheritance (vv. 12-14)?

The word Paul uses for "guarantee" here is a word used at the time in legal or commercial transactions. Suppose I wanted to buy a plot of land from you, valued at $10,000. We might agree that I would pay you the first $1,000 as a "down payment," guaranteeing the full sum to come in the future when the details were complete. The Spirit is the "down payment": part of the promised future, coming forward to meet us in the present.

12. What difference does knowing you are to receive God's inheritance in full make in your life?

PRAY

Praise God for the blessings he has given you through Jesus the Messiah and the inheritance that you will receive in full someday.

2

THE POWER OF THE KING

Ephesians 1:15-23

So how strong is it?"

My friend was showing me his new telescope. It was set up in an upstairs room, looking out toward sea.

"Well, take a look."

I had been scanning the horizon with my own small binoculars. There were a couple of ships going by. A few small fishing boats closer in. Nothing much else. I put my eye to his telescope and couldn't believe what I saw. The two ships I had seen—suddenly they were so close that I could see their names on the side, and people walking to and fro on deck. But that was only the beginning. Out beyond them, where my binoculars had registered nothing at all, were several other ships: large and small, military and commercial, including a cruise liner. The telescope seemed to have the uncanny power of making things appear out of nowhere.

OPEN

When have you experienced something unexpectedly powerful?

STUDY

1. *Read Ephesians 1:15-23.* Power is one of the great themes of Ephesians. Perhaps this is because Ephesus itself, and the surrounding area, was seen as a place of power. Certainly in social and civic terms the city was powerful, and was set to become more so. It was a major center of imperial influence in Paul's day. It was also a center of religious power. Before Paul writes about power, though, he tells his readers how thankful he is for them. Why is he grateful for his readers (vv. 15-16)?

2. How does Paul mix praise with petition when he prays (v. 17)?

3. What are his specific prayer requests for his readers (vv. 17-19)?

4. According to Paul's prayer, we acquire wisdom as we get to know God. How does knowing Jesus more help us see things differently?

5. What are some practical ways we can do that?

6. What was the greatest display of power the world has ever seen (v. 20)?

7. At the center of Paul's prayer for the church in the area, which he now reports, is his longing that they will come to realize that this same power, the power seen at Easter and now vested in Jesus, is available to them for their daily use. Far too many Christians today, and, one suspects, in Paul's day, are quite unaware that this power is there and is available. They are like I was with my friend: until I looked through his powerful telescope I simply didn't know what was out there.

   Paul doesn't imagine that all Christians will automatically be able to recognize the power of God. It will take, as he says in verse 17, a fresh gift of wisdom, of coming to see things people don't normally see. And this in turn will come about through knowing Jesus and having what Paul calls "the eyes of your innermost self" opened to God's light.

   What should and shouldn't using this power look like in our daily lives?

8. How have you experienced this power in your life?

9. What authority does Jesus have now (vv. 21-22)?

10. King Jesus as the head of the body of believers has the church as his hands and feet. It is "his body, the fullness of the one who fills all in all." How can we, his church, act as his agents within the present world?

PRAY

Thank God for the power you have through Jesus' resurrection, and ask him to help you use it in your daily life.

3

LIFE AFTER DEATH

Ephesians 2:1-10

Many years ago, I was staying for a few days in Cape Town, South Africa. Among the people I wanted to meet was an elderly man who lived on the edge of the city, in one of the outer suburbs. We arranged by telephone that I should drive out, in a rented car, and have supper with him and his wife.

He gave me detailed instructions on how to find him. Unfortunately, when I set off it was dark, and raining, and I managed to start in the wrong direction on the expressway. Since he had told me to go for ten miles or so before looking for the signs to turn off, I didn't worry until I'd gone at least twelve or fifteen miles and none of the signs were making sense. Eventually I turned off the road and asked at a garage. They hadn't heard of the district I was looking for, never mind the street. I was totally in the wrong part of the city. Only gradually, when we studied the map, did I realize my mistake. I had been driving confidently, believing I was doing the right thing, but with every minute I had been going further and further away from where I wanted to be.

OPEN

Describe a time when you chose the wrong direction, whether it was while driving, in a relationship or some other situation.

STUDY

1. *Read Ephesians 2:1-7.* We live in a world where human beings, left to themselves, not only choose the wrong direction, but remain cheerfully confident that it is in fact the right one. What forces lure or compel us to go in the wrong direction spiritually (vv. 1-2)?

   What reasons have you heard people give for the direction they're going in their life?

2. What, according to Paul, characterizes people who are going in the wrong direction (v. 3)?

3. If the problem is that the settled and habitual behavior of the whole human race leads people on the fast road toward death—the ultimate destruction of their humanness—the answer provided by God is a way through death and out into a new sort of life entirely. What has God done for us to get us on the right road (vv. 4-6)?

4. Why does God love us so much?

5. How did your own "change in direction" through Christ come about?

6. God made us alive and raised us up in Christ (vv. 4-6). What does verse 7 say God desires to accomplish by this?

Of course, lots of people who are heading at speed in the wrong direction want to think of God as a bit stingy, or mean, or small-minded—just as people who are enjoying their drive don't like it if someone tells them they're going the wrong way, and that they're about to pass the last chance to turn off and head back again. But the crucial factor here, as always, is Jesus himself. Take away his resurrection, and for all anybody knows the road to death is the only road there is. Put it back in the picture, though, and you realize two things. First, there is another way. Second, you are urgently summoned to turn round and follow it.

7. *Read Ephesians 2:8-10.* What is the means of our salvation (vv. 8-9)?

8. Paul's gospel is all about grace that is more than mere enrichment. It gives life to the dead. It is God's free, undeserved gift.

Many people think they can earn their salvation by doing good works. Do you ever feel like you need to earn God's favor or grace? If so, why do you think it's hard for you to accept his grace as a free gift?

9. Why did God save us (v. 10)?

10. The "good works" which Paul mentions in verse 10 are not the same as the "works of the law" (which he rules out in Romans) which marked people as members of the Jewish community. The "good works" are the way of life Christians must now travel in the right direction, after the disastrously wrong journey described earlier. What are some good works for which God created us?

11. Verse 10 is one of Paul's central statements of how Christians are at the center of God's new creation. We are, he says, God's workmanship. This word sometimes has an artistic ring to it. It may be hinting that what God has done to us in King Jesus is a work of art, like a poem or sculpture. Or perhaps, granted what he goes on to say, we are like a musical score; and the music, which we now have to play, is the genuine way of being human, laid out before us in God's gracious design, so that we can follow it. They are the way of life which he will describe more fully in chapters 4—6.

How do you respond to the idea that you are God's artistic creation?

PRAY

Thank God for providing salvation by grace and not expecting you to be good enough or do enough to earn it. Ask him to show you what good works you can do this week to demonstrate your salvation.

4

WELCOME TO THE FAMILY

Ephesians 2:11-22

One of the greatest worldwide problems of our time is the plight of refugees and asylum-seekers. People in the West sometimes try to pretend that the world is now a civilized place where most people can go about their business in peace, and at least relative prosperity. But the evidence suggests that is overoptimistic. More people than ever, it seems, are displaced from homes and homelands, and find themselves wandering the world in search of somewhere to live. The countries where they arrive are often overwhelmed, and find that their resources, and their patience, are under strain, despite feeling sympathetic to people who have often suffered a great deal.

What refugees want above all, assuming that they can never return to their original homes, is to be accepted into a new community where they can rebuild their lives and their families. And the ultimate sign of that acceptance is to receive citizenship in the country they have adopted as their own. Their new passport is often their proudest possession. At last they can hold their heads up and build a new sense of identity. They have arrived. They belong.

OPEN

When have you sought to be part of a new group: a new country, a circle of friends at school or work, or a club? Describe your experience.

STUDY

1. *Read Ephesians 2:11-16.* Spiritually, we become part of a new group too. How does Paul describe Gentiles before they became part of this new group (vv. 11-13)?

   The word Paul uses in verse 12 to describe them as having no god is the word from which we get our word *atheists.* This is ironic, because that's what Gentiles used to call Jews, and then came to call Christians as well, since neither Jews nor Christians had statues of their gods. Neither, so far as the Gentile eye could see, offered animal sacrifice, consulted oracles or did any of the other things that pagans associated with worship of their gods. Paul, boldly standing on the same ground as Jewish writers of the same period, declares that the pagan gods are actually non-gods. Those who think they worship them are worshiping something that doesn't really exist.

2. What did Jesus do specifically for Gentiles on the one hand (vv. 12-14) and for Jewish people on the other (vv. 14-15)?

3. Consider how those receiving this letter from Paul might have reacted to these verses. How easy or difficult do you think it was for

them to live out the oneness they were called to as fellow believers in Christ?

4. Why did God do all this (v. 16)?

Today's church may no longer face the question of the integration of Jew and Gentile into a single family, though there are places where that is still a major issue. But we face, quite urgently, the question which Paul would insist on as a major priority. If our churches are still divided in any way along racial or cultural lines, he would say that our gospel, our very grasp of the meaning of Jesus' death, is called into question.

5. What challenges often come up when groups of people who used to be separate come together to form one group?

6. How well are different groups in your church or Christian fellowship included in a single body? Explain.

7. What changes do you need to make to encourage more openness to include others who are different in your church?

8. How, in light of Ephesians 2:1-3 (and ahead in 4:17-24), can we tell the difference between the "differences" which we must disregard

within the church and the "differences" which are still important?

9. *Read Ephesians 2:17-22.* How did Jesus' life and death bring peace for both Jews and Gentiles (vv. 17-18)?

10. In what ways have you experienced this peace?

11. Paul describes our equality in Jesus with three images: *citizens, family* and *building.* How is each of these three words descriptive of people before and after they become Christians (vv. 19-22)?

The closing verses of the chapter take one of the central symbols of Judaism and turn it inside out. The temple in Jerusalem was not only the religious heart of the nation, and the place of pilgrimage of Jews throughout the world. It was also the political, social, musical and cultural heart of Jerusalem—as well as the place of celebration and feasting. The reason for all this was, of course, that Israel's God had promised to live there. It was, many believed, the place where earth and heaven met.

But now Paul is declaring that the living God is constructing a new temple. It consists not of stones, arches, pillars and altars, but of human beings. Some Jews had already explored the idea that a community, rather than a building, might be the place where God would really and truly take up his residence. But until Paul nobody had said anything quite like this.

12. Let's look again at each of these three images—citizens, family members and a building. What are the implications for being a citizen of God's kingdom?

13. How should our interactions with each other be different because we are members of God's family?

PRAY

Thank God for the opportunity to be part of his family, and ask him to use you to make others feel welcomed into it.

GOD'S SECRET PLAN
REVEALED

Ephesians 3:1-13

Naomi had started a small dressmaking business. The brightly colored fabrics of her part of Africa were popular not only in the surrounding district but also, she'd heard, in foreign countries.

She employed two women to help with the dressmaking, and a young man to travel to the city to buy supplies and sell the finished products. Together they worked hard, and soon they had more orders than they could easily complete. Naomi hired two more helpers.

One day one of the women said, "You know, I wonder if we could make other things as well as dresses? Curtains? Covers for chairs? Things like that?"

The others agreed enthusiastically.

Naomi smiled. She went to her desk and took out a sealed envelope, which had a date written across the seal—the day on which she started the business. She passed the envelope to the woman who had asked the question.

"Open it, and read it out."

She opened the envelope and read the paper. It contained the plan for a larger business that would make the wonderful fabrics into all sorts of things people might want in their homes.

"I've kept it a secret all this time," said Naomi. "I knew if I told you from the start you'd say I was daydreaming and then you'd have started daydreaming yourselves. We had to prove we could make dresses first. But this is what I planned all along. Let's do it!"

OPEN

What is one dream you've had that came to fruition?

STUDY

1. *Read Ephesians 3:1-13.* Paul's picture of God in this passage is a bit like the picture of Naomi. What was God's secret plan (vv. 1-6)?

2. How did he reveal his plan (vv. 2-5)?

3. What three great privileges did the Gentiles attain (together with the Jews) in this plan (v. 6)?

Fancy hearing the news that a family down the street has come into a large and wealthy inheritance—and then being told that you are to become full members of that family, with instant privileges identical to theirs! That's the situation that Christian Gentiles now find themselves in.

4. How did God accomplish this plan (v. 7)?

5. What does this plan of God's—the plan itself, the fact that God kept it hidden and then revealed it, the way he accomplished it—reveal about the character of God?

6. What task did God give Paul (vv. 8-9)?

Paul is the one chosen by God to pioneer the plan. In terms of Naomi and her dressmaking business, he hadn't been expecting the localized and family-based company (Israel) to expand like this (to reach out to include non-Jews on equal terms).

7. How does Paul describe God's secret plan (v. 10)?

The heart of the present passage is verse 10, which is one of the New Testament's most powerful statements of the reason for the church's existence: the rulers and authorities must be confronted with God's wisdom, in all its rich variety, and this is to happen through the church! Not, we should quickly add, through what the church *says,* though that is vital as well. Rather, through what the church *is,* namely, the community in which men, women and children of every race, color, social and cultural background come together in glad worship of the one true God.

It is precisely this many-sided, many-colored, many-splendored identity of the church that makes the point. God's wisdom, Paul is saying, is like that too: like a many-faceted diamond which twinkles and sparkles with all the colors in the rainbow. The "rulers and authorities," however—both the earthly authorities and their shadowy heavenly counterparts—always tend to create societies and social structures in their own flat, boring image, monochrome, uniform and one-dimensional. Worse: they tend to marginalize or kill people or groups who don't fit their narrow band of acceptability. The church is to be, by the very fact of its existence, a warning to them that their time is up, and an announcement to the world that there is a different way to be human.

8. How can your Christian fellowship explore the riches of Christ described by Paul?

9. What does it mean to approach God with confidence and assurance (vv. 11-12)?

10. How can these two characteristics change the prayer life of your Christian community?

11. Why does Paul describe his sufferings as his readers' "glory" (v. 13)?

12. The fact that Paul is in prison is a sign that the Christian way is indeed posing a decisive threat to the rule of evil in the world. In what

specific ways can we, as God's people, challenge the power of evil today in a way that provokes a reaction?

PRAY

Thank God for revealing his secret plan and for the incredible riches he has given you in Christ.

Praise God for the diversity of people and cultures in his church. Ask that this diversity might grow to fulfill its purpose of making God's wisdom known around the world.

6

POWER AND LOVE

Ephesians 3:14-21

Love and power, power and love; these are the themes of perhaps two-thirds of the novels, plays and poems ever written. The love of power has laid waste continents and empires. The power of love has driven weak people to do powerful things—and, not infrequently, powerful people to do foolish things. These are the forces which shape our lives, our homes, our countries, our politics, our world.

OPEN

What examples of the love of power or the power of love have you seen or experienced?

STUDY

1. *Read Ephesians 3:14-21.* Power and love are the themes that run through the great prayer that Paul prays for the young Christians to whom he is writing. What is Paul's frame of mind when he prays this prayer (vv. 14-15)?

There is nothing perfunctory about Paul's worship and prayer. One gets the sense, here and elsewhere, that his life revolved around it. This, we may suppose, is part of the secret of the extraordinary power that seemed to flow through his preaching, his pastoral work and his writing.

The church in the Western world has perhaps allowed itself to be lulled into thinking that prayer and action are at opposite ends of the scale of Christian activity. On the contrary. Those who want their actions to be effective for God's kingdom should redouble their time and effort in prayer. Prayer brings together love and power: the relation of love that grows up between God and the person who prays, and the flowing of power from God to, and especially *through*, that person.

That is what Paul's prayer here is all about. Essentially, it is a prayer that the young Christians may discover the heart of what it means to be a Christian.

2. Paul's first request is that God would strengthen and empower them in their inner beings (v. 16). What resources does God have to do this?

3. What does it mean to be strengthened "in your inner being"?

4. What are Paul's next prayer requests (v. 17)?

5. What characterizes someone in whom King Jesus dwells?

People talk easily, perhaps too easily, about "inviting Jesus into your heart," or "having Jesus in your heart." The danger here is that it's easy for people, particularly when they are soaked in the culture of Western-style individualism, to imagine that being a Christian consists simply in being able to feel, or believe, that Jesus has somehow taken up residence within. In fact, Paul speaks far more often of Christians being "in Christ" than of Christ being "in Christians." It's important to see our individual experience within the larger picture of our membership in God's family in the Messiah, within the worldwide plan Paul has been talking of in these three chapters.

6. Why does Paul pray that love would be their root, their firm foundation?

7. Finally, Paul prays that they will know God's love. How does he describe that love (vv. 18-19)?

8. What difference can a fuller understanding of God's love make in specific ways, like how we interact with others, how we view ourselves, how we manage our finances and so forth?

9. How does this prayer come back in verse 19 to where it stopped in 1:23?

10. How are verses 20-21 an appropriate ending to this prayer?

11. How are Paul's prayers similar to or different from the kinds of prayers you or those in your community pray?

12. What might God do in and through you as a community?

   As an individual?

PRAY

Reflect on the fact that God is perfectly capable of doubling, trebling, going so far beyond what we think he might do. This isn't a magic trick. God's power is not ours to do what we like with.

   Pray verses 16-21, personalizing them, putting yourself, fellow Christians and your church in the prayer by name.

7

Living Our Calling

Ephesians 4:1-16

If you buy a new car, what's the first thing you do?

Do you sit down for an hour and read through the manual, to make sure you know every little detail about it before you take to the road? Or do you at once get behind the wheel and go for a drive, enjoying all the things the car can do and not worrying about the details, at least for the moment? In the same way, it's notorious that when people buy a new computer they tend to operate it first and read the instruction manual afterward.

The trouble is, of course, that things go wrong with machinery. They may go wrong even quicker if you don't read the instructions. But most people will at least keep the instruction book handy and refer to it from time to time to see how the machine was meant to behave, what the fundamental instructions were and what needs to be done to ensure that it remains at maximum efficiency.

OPEN

When you buy something that comes with instructions, do you read the instructions? Why or why not?

STUDY

1. *Read Ephesians 4:1-6.* In this section, which opens the second half of the letter, Paul takes his readers back to the fundamental instructions on living the Christian life. He reminds them how they began and what it was all about. The Christian life begins with a calling. He isn't referring to the specific "calling" or "vocation" that different Christians have—teacher, nurse, business leader and so forth. What elements comprise that calling to faith Paul has in mind here (vv. 1-5)?

2. How can we "bear with one another in love" (v. 2)?

3. Describe the unity that God has given us with other believers (locally or around the world) even when we have differences with them (vv. 3-6).

4. What threatens unity in your Christian community?

5. How can we maintain and guard this unity we have with other believers?

It may be hard for Christians today to grasp just how central this unity was to Paul's vision of the church. We have grown accustomed to so many divisions within the worldwide church. Sometimes customs and practices have grown up in churches which are so different that members of one have difficulty recognizing members of another as fellow Christians. Sometimes, indeed, the boundaries *are* blurred, and it may be possible for a church to wander off course so much that its claim to be loyal to Jesus Christ is seriously called into question.

But whatever position we take today, the one thing we can't do is to pretend that this isn't a central and vital issue. Unless we are working to maintain, defend and develop the unity we already enjoy, and to overcome, demolish and put behind us the disunity we still find ourselves in, we can scarcely claim to be following Paul's teaching.

6. What is the "single hope" that goes with our call (vv. 4-6)?

At every moment, in every decision, with every word and action, Christians are to be aware that the call to follow Jesus the Messiah and give him their complete loyalty takes precedence over everything else.

7. *Read Ephesians 4:7-16.* Some diversity exists with the unity Paul emphasizes in the previous verses. What is this diversity (vv. 7, 11)?

8. Why does God give some believers the particular leadership gifts mentioned in verses 11-12?

The list of offices in verse 11 is not exhaustive. Elsewhere Paul adds others. But these five were crucial to the establishment of the first generation of the church. Apostles were witnesses to the resurrection; since the resurrection is the foundation of the church, the testimony of those who had seen the risen Jesus was the first Christian preaching. Early Christian prophets spoke in the name of the Lord, guiding and directing the church especially in the time before the New Testament was written. Evangelists announced to the surprised world that the crucified Jesus was risen from the dead, and was both Israel's Messiah and the world's true Lord. Pastors looked after the young churches; teachers developed and trained their understanding. They did this not least by setting out the many ways in which believing allegiance to Jesus linked Christians into the whole story and life of Israel, building on the promises of the Old Testament.

9. It's not the particular gift that matters; it's using the gift that's important. What are the results of using the ministry gifts God gives us (vv. 13-16)?

10. Based on the images Paul uses in verse 14, what seem to have been the main obstacles to his readers' faith in Jesus?

11. Where does your church need to grow toward maturity?

12. How can you use the gifts God has given you to enable this to take place?

PRAY

Thank God for your calling to faith and the body of believers he has put you in. Ask for his help to maintain unity in your body and promote growth through the use of your gift(s).

NOTE ON EPHESIANS 4:8-10

Before Paul gives his list of gifts Jesus has given to his church, Paul quotes Psalm 68:18. This would have reminded first-century Jews of Moses going up Mount Sinai and coming down with the stone tablets of the law after he had rescued Israel from captivity in Egypt. Paul sees a parallel in Jesus. After "the new Exodus" had been achieved in Christ's death and resurrection, setting the human race free from bondage to sin and death, Jesus "went up" to the heavenly realm where he now reigns. Intead of coming down again with the law, as Moses had done, Jesus "returned" in the person of the Spirit, through whom different gifts are now showered on the church.

8

OFF WITH THE OLD,
ON WITH THE NEW

Ephesians 4:17—5:2

We couldn't understand why the agency was being so unhelpful.

We had answered the advertisement and were eager to rent the apartment that we had been offered. There were some minor problems, but nothing too difficult to sort out. But every time we telephoned we spoke to a different person, and they never seemed to understand what was happening. They gave different answers each time we asked the questions. They quoted us different rates. The worst thing was that they didn't really seem to care whether we rented the place or not.

When we finally visited the office it became clear. The secretaries and assistants we had been speaking to on the telephone were bright enough. They obviously would have liked to be helpful. But the manager—who had never talked to us himself—was impossible. He was inefficient, haphazard, and we suspected he had a drink problem. But he covered it all up by being a bully. He shouted at his employees and gave them different directions every day. No wonder they hadn't been able to help us much. Only by confronting him directly and making him face the issues could we begin to sort everything out.

When we begin to get to grips with the wrong way and the right way to live a truly human life, it's no good starting with the junior members of the establishment. People often suppose that Christian behavior is simply a matter of getting your body to do certain things and not do certain other things. That's like us trying to do business with the assistants rather than directly with the incompetent manager. Paul makes it clear in this passage that you've got to go about it the other way round. And the incompetent manager isn't the human body. It's the human mind.

OPEN

When it comes to changing our behavior, would you agree that the mind is the place to begin rather than the body? Explain.

STUDY

1. *Read Ephesians 4:17-24.* How does Paul describe the pagan mind and heart (4:17-18)?

2. What behavior resulted from that thinking (4:19)?

3. How is this thinking and behavior similar to our culture today?

4. In contrast, what teaching did the believers receive (4:20-24)?

Paul is urging the young Christians that they allow this teaching of Jesus to have its full effect in their lives. Now that they are "in Christ," they have the responsibility, in the power of the Spirit, to take off the old lifestyle, the old way of being human, like someone stripping off a shabby and worn suit of clothing. It may have become comfortable. You may be used to it, and even quite like it. Familiar old clothes are often like that, and brand new ones often feel a bit strange. But if you want to live as a new person in and for the king, the old suit of clothes has to come off, and the new one has to go on.

5. How can we be "renewed in the spirit of our mind" (4:23)?

6. *Read Ephesians 4:25—5:2.* What are the sins Paul says we are to put off?

7. What new behaviors are we to put on instead, and what reason does Paul give for each?

8. How prevalent are these "new behaviors" in our culture today? Why do you think that is?

9. What's the overriding reason to change our thinking in order to change our behavior (4:30)?

The word Paul uses for "God's mark" could refer to the "seal" or official stamp on a document or package, marking it out for a particular use or occasion. The mark indicates who it belongs to and what it's for. If we are marked out by the Spirit's personal presence living in us, think how sad it makes that Spirit if we behave in ways which don't reflect the life and love of God.

10. Which of these old ways of thinking and behaving do you need to put off?

11. Paul says we should imitate God (5:1-2). How can we do that?

12. Scan through the "new behaviors" again that are found at the end of Ephesians 4, but this time read them as a description of how God acts toward us. How does that make you think and feel differently about the whole passage?

PRAY

Praise God for how he acts toward you. Ask God to show you areas of thinking and behavior that are wrong and how you can change them, so you can imitate him.

WALKING IN THE LIGHT

Ephesians 5:3-20

The poster in the college gateway had one large word in the middle of it: SEX. Underneath, in small print, it said, "Now you're interested, how about joining the College Rowing Club?" Whoever designed the poster wasn't suggesting that taking up rowing had anything to do with sex. They were simply exploiting the fact that in contemporary Western society people are so obsessed with sex that the very word attracts people's attention. Anything associated with it seems attractive as well.

OPEN

What is a recent ad you've seen or heard that uses sex to sell something?

How did you respond to it?

STUDY

1. *Read Ephesians 5:3-10.* In many ways the world of Paul's day wasn't much different from ours today, particularly in the cities where he spent most of his time. Casual sex and all kinds of curious practices associated with it seem to have flourished. What is Paul's remedy for immorality (vv. 3-4, 7)?

2. What reasons does Paul give for this remedy (vv. 3, 5-6)?

Paul has a way of cutting to the heart of the issue. Don't be fooled, he says. There are a lot of empty words out there—words, that is, which sound big and important, which echo and resonate in our culture, but which have nothing inside them, no life, no truth. Precisely because sex is a good, joyous and important gift of God's creation; precisely because it is the means of tenderness and intimacy between husband and wife, as well as the means of God-given procreation; precisely because it is the occasion for great blessing and emotional fulfillment; because of all these, people on the road to genuinely human existence promised in Christ must avoid all cheap imitations.

Casual sex is a parody of the real thing—like drinking from a muddy stream instead of fresh, clear water, or like listening to a symphony from a damaged audio file when a world-class orchestra is playing in the theater around the corner.

3. What has influenced your view of sex?

4. Has your view changed at all through the years? If so, explain.

5. In contrast to the culture of Paul's day, how are we to behave (vv. 8-10)?

6. *Read Ephesians 5:11-20.* What should our attitude be toward "the works of darkness" (v. 11)?

7. What are some works of darkness we encounter on a regular basis?

8. How can we expose those works of darkness to the light, or truth (vv. 12-14)?

9. What commands does Paul give for how believers are to conduct themselves (vv. 15-20)?

10. What is one practical way you can live out each of Paul's commands?

11. Based on verse 19, what role did psalms and hymns and spiritual songs seem to play in Paul's life?

12. How is that similar to or different from how hymns and choruses are used today?

13. If you don't want your garden to grow weeds, one of the best ways is to keep it well stocked with strong, sturdy flowers and shrubs. If you don't want your mind and heart to go wandering off into the realms of darkness, one of the best ways is to keep them well stocked with wise and thankful themes, so that words of comfort, guidance and good judgment come bubbling up unbidden from the memory and subconscious. Hymns and psalms today can still provide exactly this kind of Christian nurture.

    The singing that Paul has in mind is the ultimate antidote to living in the darkness of immorality that pervades the surrounding world. Yet again his emphasis is on the mind, and the need for wisdom. It is vital not to slide along through life in a general foolish haze, hoping things will work out all right but not being prepared to think them through, to figure out where this or that type of behavior will really lead.

    How have hymns and spiritual songs been important to you?

PRAY

Ask God to fill your heart, mind and imagination with his truth, so you can live in a way that is pleasing to him.

NEW RELATIONSHIPS

Ephesians 5:21—6:9

Families, like the marriage relationship, have often been seen in our culture as oppressive and enslaving. We all know of homes where this seems to be the case. But we shouldn't make the mistake of thinking that because some families get it horribly wrong, it isn't possible to get it right, at least some of the time. Just because the garden grows weeds, we shouldn't pave it over with concrete. Just because there are oppressive families, that's no reason to dismiss family life altogether.

On the contrary, marriage and the family were designed as the place of love, security, affirmation and new energy; but they can become a place of fear and bondage. The worst is the corruption of the best.

OPEN

Briefly describe your ideal marriage, family or relationship with co-workers?

STUDY

1. *Read Ephesians 5:21.* Paul addresses all these types of relationships

when he writes to the Ephesians. He prefaces his instructions with a general, overriding one. What attitude are we to have toward others?

2. What should submission look like in daily life?

3. *Read Ephesians 5:22-33.* Why does Paul tell wives to submit to their husbands (5:22-24)?

4. How does remembering that a wife is really submitting to the Lord affect submission to a husband?

5. How are husbands, in turn, to treat their wives (5:25-33)?

6. How does comparing a husband's love for his wife to how the Messiah loved the church remove any danger of the husband abusing the wife's submission?

7. Paul assumes, as do most cultures, that there are significant differences between men and women, differences that go far beyond mere biological and reproductive function. Their relations and roles must therefore be mutually complementary, rather than identical. Equality in voting rights, and in employment opportunities and re-

muneration, should not be taken to imply such identity. And, within marriage, the guideline is clear. The husband is to take the lead—though he is to do so fully mindful of the self-sacrificial model which the Messiah has provided. The church became the Messiah's bride, not by being dragged off unwillingly by force, but because he gave himself totally and utterly for her. As soon as "taking the lead" becomes bullying or arrogant, the whole thing collapses.

If this guideline still seems outrageous in today's culture, we should ask ourselves: do our modern societies, in which marriage is often a tragedy or a joke, really offer a better model of how to do it? Does the specter of broken homes littering modern Western culture indicate that we've got it right and can tell the rest of human history how we finally resolved the battle of the sexes? Or does it indicate that we still need to do some rethinking somewhere?

What are some practical ways husbands and wives can live out 5:33?

8. *Read Ephesians 6:1-9.* What does it mean for children to obey and honor their parents (6:1-3)?

9. How can fathers—and mothers—practice the commands for them in verse 4?

10. Paul could no more envisage a world without slavery than we can envisage a world without electricity. The way Paul's world worked was through slaves taking a vital place in most households except those of the very poor. If Paul were writing this letter today, he would address his instructions to employees and employers.

How are slaves, or employees, to do their work (6:5-8)?

11. In turn, how are masters, or employers, to treat their slaves, or employees (6:9)?

The remarkable thing about Ephesians 6:1-9, both the commands to children and parents and those to slaves and masters, is that the children and slaves evidently have, in Paul's eyes, what we would call "rights" as well as the parents and masters. When ancient philosophers drew up codes of behavior, as they did from time to time, the weight was always the other way round. Slaves and children were to be obedient, and that was the end of it. Now Paul insists on a mutual responsibility.

The final part of 6:9 says it all: God doesn't have favorites based on position or wealth or ethnic origin.

12. Choose one role from this study: husband, wife, parent, child, employer, employee. When is it hard for you to follow Paul's instructions for that role, and what would help you change?

PRAY

Thank God that we can have new relationships through faith in Messiah. Ask him to help you live according to Paul's instructions here.

Dressed for the Battle

Ephesians 6:10-24

For some reason, almost whenever I write about passages dealing with spiritual warfare, I run into problems. One time a workman outside the house drove a nail through a main electricity cable, and I lost half an hour's writing on the word processor. Sometimes domestic crises suddenly arise and distract me. Today the computer jammed completely just when I was about to begin writing. I have come to accept this as normal—and to be grateful that this is all that has happened. So far.

I don't claim that this of itself makes my work anything special. But I have noticed, over the years, that the topic of spiritual warfare is itself the subject of spiritual warfare. It is as though certain hidden forces would much rather we didn't talk about it, or that we swept it under the carpet. As C. S. Lewis says in the introduction to his famous *Screwtape Letters,* the general public prefers either to ignore the forces of evil altogether or to take an unhealthy interest in everything demonic, which can be just as bad in the long run.

OPEN

Describe a time when you were engaged in some kind of spiritual battle and how you handled it.

STUDY

1. *Read Ephesians 6:10-17.* What we have in this passage, and what I believe is required again and again as Christians face the daily and yearly battle for the kingdom, is a sober, realistic assessment both of the struggle we are engaged in and of the weapons at our disposal. What strength do we have for this battle (v. 10)?

2. What kind of warfare are we engaged in (vv. 11-12)?

Sometimes the attack will take the frontal form of actual authorities in towns and cities who try to prevent Christians from spreading the message. Sometimes it will take the more oblique form of persuading Christians to invest time and energy in irrelevant side issues, or to become fascinated by distorted teaching. Sometimes it will be simply the age-old temptations of money, sex and power. But in each case what individuals and the whole church must do is, first, to recognize that attacks are coming; second, to learn how to put on the complete armor which God offers; and, third, to stand firm and undismayed.

3. To win the battles, God has provided a set of armor for us (vv. 13-17). Identify the six pieces of armor and a specific way we might use each today.

4. In what way is the sword of the Spirit, which is the word of God, an offensive weapon in contrast to the other defensive weapons?

The "word" in verse 17 is clearly the same as in 5:26, that is, the word of the gospel through which God accomplishes his powerful, cleansing work in people's hearts and lives.

5. Which piece of armor is difficult for you to utilize and why?

6. How can you learn to actively "take up" that weapon?

7. *Read Ephesians 6:18-20.* The final weapon, if it is to be classed as one, is prayer. How does prayer help us fight spiritual battles (v. 18)?

8. How is prayer hard work for you (v. 18)?

9. What does Paul ask his readers to pray about for him (vv. 19-20)?

The word Paul uses in verse 20 for "boldly" could almost mean "brazenly." He is settled in his mind that he will go on talking about King Jesus, his victory over death, and his present and future kingdom, no matter what happens. But he knows that unless people are praying for him he won't be able to do it, and it wouldn't mean anything if he did.

So having begun the letter with an extended prayer, and then an extensive report of his own prayers for the young Christians in the area, he now finishes it with the urgent request that they join him in this ministry.

10. How are these requests relevant for ourselves and other believers today?

11. *Read Ephesians 6:21-24.* Why does Paul include these personal notes about Tychicus (vv. 21-22)?

12. Why do you think Paul emphasizes peace in his closing greeting (vv. 23-24)?

Peace, here as elsewhere, is bound up closely with love and faith. It comes from the one true God, the Father, and the Lord, King Jesus, and it comes as a sure blessing on those whose love for this same Jesus will outlast death itself. That, after all, is what being a Christian is all about: loving Jesus with an undying love, in response to his dying love for us.

PRAY

Thank God for providing this armor for the battles you encounter, and ask him to help you remember to use it, especially prayer.

Guidelines for Leaders

My grace is sufficient for you.
(2 Corinthians 12:9)

If leading a small group is something new for you, don't worry. These sessions are designed to flow naturally and be led easily. You may even find that the studies seem to lead themselves!

This study guide is flexible. You can use it with a variety of groups—students, professionals, coworkers, friends, neighborhood or church groups. Each study takes forty-five to sixty minutes in a group setting.

You don't need to be an expert on the Bible or a trained teacher to lead a small group. These guides are designed to facilitate a group's discussion, not a leader's presentation. Guiding group members to discover together what the Bible has to say and to listen together for God's guidance will help them remember much more than a lecture would.

There are some important facts to know about group dynamics and encouraging discussion. The suggestions listed below should equip you to effectively and enjoyably fulfill your role as leader.

PREPARING FOR THE STUDY

1. Ask God to help you understand and apply the passage in your own life. Unless this happens, you will not be prepared to lead others. Pray too for the various members of the group. Ask God to open

your hearts to the message of his Word and motivate you to action.

2. Read the introduction to the entire guide to get an overview of the topics that will be explored.

3. As you begin each study, read and reread the assigned Bible passage to familiarize yourself with it. This study guide is based on the For Everyone series on the New Testament (published by SPCK and Westminster John Knox). It will help you and the group if you have on hand a copy of the companion volume from the For Everyone series both for the translation of the passage found there and for further insight into the passage.

4. Carefully work through each question in the study. Spend time in meditation and reflection as you consider how to respond.

5. Write your thoughts and responses in the space provided in the study guide. This will help you to express your understanding of the passage clearly.

6. It may help to have a Bible dictionary handy. Use it to look up any unfamiliar words, names or places. The glossary at the end of each New Testament for Everyone commentary may likewise be helpful for keeping discussion moving.

7. Reflect seriously on how you need to apply the Scripture to your life. Remember that the group members will follow your lead in responding to the studies. They will not go any deeper than you do.

LEADING THE STUDY

1. At the beginning of your first time together, explain that these studies are meant to be discussions, not lectures. Encourage the members of the group to participate. However, do not put pressure on those who may be hesitant to speak—especially during the first few sessions.

2. Be sure that everyone in your group has a study guide. Encourage the group to prepare beforehand for each discussion by reading the introduction to the guide and by working through the questions in each study.

3. Begin each study on time. Open with prayer, asking God to help the group to understand and apply the passage.

4. Have a group member read aloud the introduction at the beginning of the discussion.

5. Discuss the "Open" question before the Bible passage is read. The "Open" question introduces the theme of the study and helps group members to begin to open up, and can reveal where our thoughts and feelings need to be transformed by Scripture. Reading the passage first will tend to color the honest reactions people would otherwise give—because they are, of course, supposed to think the way the Bible does. Encourage as many members as possible to respond to the "Open" question, and be ready to get the discussion going with your own response.

6. Have a group member read aloud the passage to be studied as indicated in the guide.

7. The study questions are designed to be read aloud just as they are written. You may, however, prefer to express them in your own words.

   There may be times when it is appropriate to deviate from the study guide. For example, a question may have already been answered. If so, move on to the next question. Or someone may raise an important question not covered in the guide. Take time to discuss it, but try to keep the group from going off on tangents.

8. Avoid answering your own questions. An eager group quickly becomes passive and silent if members think the leader will do most of the talking. If necessary repeat or rephrase the question until it is clearly understood, or refer to the commentary woven into the guide to clarify the context or meaning.

9. Don't be afraid of silence in response to the discussion questions. People may need time to think about the question before formulating their answers.

10. Don't be content with just one answer. Ask, "What do the rest of you think?" or "Anything else?" until several people have given answers to the question.

11. Try to be affirming whenever possible. Affirm participation. Never reject an answer; if it is clearly off-base, ask, "Which verse led you to that conclusion?" or again, "What do the rest of you think?"

12. Don't expect every answer to be addressed to you, even though this will probably happen at first. As group members become more at ease, they will begin to truly interact with each other. This is one sign of healthy discussion.

13. Don't be afraid of controversy. It can be very stimulating. If you don't resolve an issue completely, don't be frustrated. Explain that the group will move on and God may enlighten all of you in later sessions.

14. Periodically summarize what the group has said about the passage. This helps to draw together the various ideas mentioned and gives continuity to the study. But don't preach.

15. Conclude your time together with the prayer suggestion at the end of the study, adapting it to your group's particular needs as appropriate. Ask for God's help in following through on the applications you've identified.

16. End on time.

Many more suggestions and helps for studying a passage or guiding discussion can be found in *How to Lead a LifeGuide Bible Study* and *The Big Book on Small Groups* (both from InterVarsity Press/USA).

Other InterVarsity Press Resources from N. T. Wright

The Challenge of Jesus
N. T. Wright offers clarity and a full accounting of the facts of the life and teachings of Jesus, revealing how the Son of God was also solidly planted in first-century Palestine. *978-0-8308-2200-3, 202 pages, hardcover*

Resurrection
This 50-minute DVD confronts the most startling claim of Christianity—that Jesus rose from the dead. Shot on location in Israel, Greece and England, N. T. Wright presents the political, historical and theological issues of Jesus' day and today regarding this claim. Wright brings clarity and insight to one of the most profound mysteries in human history. Study guide included.
978-0-8308-3435-8, DVD

Evil and the Justice of God
N. T. Wright explores all aspects of evil and how it presents itself in society today. Fully grounded in the story of the Old and New Testaments, this presentation is provocative and hopeful; a fascinating analysis of and response to the fundamental question of evil and justice that faces believers.
978-0-8308-3398-6, 176 pages, hardcover

Evil
Filmed in Israel, South Africa and England, this 50-minute DVD confronts some of the major "evil" issues of our time—from tsunamis to AIDS—and puts them under the biblical spotlight. N. T. Wright says there is a solution to the problem of evil, if only we have the honesty and courage to name it and understand it for what it is. Study guide included. *978-0-8308-3434-1, DVD*

Justification: God's Plan and Paul's Vision
In this comprehensive account and defense of the crucial doctrine of justification, Wright also responds to critics who have challenged what has come to be called the new perspective. Ultimately, he provides a chance for those in the middle of and on both sides of the debate to interact directly with his views and form their own conclusions. *978-0-8308-3863-9, 279 pages, hardcover*

Colossians and Philemon
In Colossians, Paul presents Christ as "the firstborn over all creation," and appeals to his readers to seek a maturity found only Christ. In Philemon, Paul appeals to a fellow believer to receive a runaway slave in love and forgiveness. In this volume N. T. Wright offers comment on both of these important books.
978-0-8308-4242-1, 199 pages, paperback